FUZZY BRAINS

God Talk

Editing and Production Team:
Gregory C. Benoit, James F. Couch, Jr.,
Ashley Benedict, Margaret Harris, Scott Lee

SERENDIPITY
H O U S E

N A S H V I L L E ,   T N

Published by Serendipity House Publishers
Nashville, Tennessee

International Standard Book Number: 1-57494-115-1

ACKNOWLEDGMENTS

Scripture quotations are taken from the
Holman Christian Standard Bible,
© Copyright 2000 by Holman Bible Publishers. Used by permission.

To Zondervan Bible Publishers for permission to use the NIV text,
The Holy Bible, New International Bible Society.
© 1973, 1978, 1984 by International Bible Society.
Used by permission of Zondervan Bible Publishers.

03 04 05 06 07 08 / 10 9 8 7 6 5 4 3 2 1

Nashville, Tennessee
1-800-525-9563
www.serendipityhouse.com

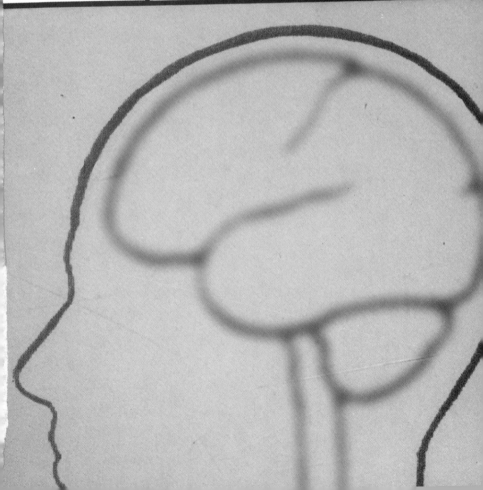

TABLE OF CONTENTS

SERENDIPITY

God Talk

The Serendipity God Talk Bible studies are designed for use by those who are lead-ing small groups of young people in their study of God's Word. These books are somewhat different from other group study guides in that they actually are not group study guides; they are more of a leader's Bible study kit, a resource tool to help a Bible study leader build a seven-week Bible study custom-tailored to meet the needs of the group.

This book is intended to be a flexible study tool for youth leaders to use in helping young people deal with the realities of modern life. They are topical studies, deal-ing with issues such as family problems, self-esteem, existential despair, anger and aggression, sexual temptation, confusion about religion, inconsistencies in our cul-ture, and many other struggles that are so common among teenagers.

This book is not intended to be a step-by-step study guide that a group reads through together. Rather, it is intended to be a tool for the leader to use to address pertinent questions and issues, turning to the Bible for the true answers. It pro-vides Scripture passages to study, probing questions to ask, directions that the dis-cussions might take, ideas for activities that make the study fun, and background information that will help make the Scriptures understandable in the 21st century.

WHAT THIS IS

Each study opens with an introduction that will offer some suggestions for what direction the discussion might take. Following this are a series of resources that a leader can use in planning out the week's study.

ACTIVITIES

This is the hands-on stuff, the opening activity that gets the group laughing together and helps them feel comfortable. There are generally two activity ideas. These ideas can also help to suggest your own ideas for activities that you create.

ICEBREAKERS

This is the "icebreaker" section, the transition time from entertaining activity toward more serious discussion. It normally offers three icebreaker questions which are very general in nature and help the group to move toward a serious consideration of God's Word.

SCRIPTURE READING

A Scripture passage is given, and the text is included for convenience. (Because the reading is usually broken into parts for several group members to read, you may copy the Scripture text for each member of the group.)

DISCUSSION QUESTIONS

This section digs into the Bible study. The Scripture passage is followed by four to six probing questions in two different categories which encourage the group to look closely at what God's Word has to say on the topic of discussion. There are two types

of questions here: factual, interpretive (or "head") questions which help the group to understand the passage; and practical, application (or "heart") questions that ask the group members to consider how they will put the ideas into practice in their own lives.

CARING TIME

The "feet" of any philosophical study is the act of putting ideas into practice. In this final section the leader will find some suggestions on possible questions to ask of the group, questions that will urge each person to plan on putting into practice the ideas that have been studied. It is essential that the group spend some time in prayer during this portion of the meeting. At times suggestions will be offered to guide the prayer. Make sure you are sensitive to the concerns that the group members share during the discussions. Incorporate these concerns into the prayer time.

NEXT WEEK

Each study concludes with an overview of what will be studied in the next session. This also includes a "heads up," a note to the leader of anything that may require any advanced preparation, such as things to ask the group members to bring with them next week.

NOTES.

Finally, additional notes are provided which will assist the leader in understanding such issues as the culture in which the story is taking place, background on the people in the story, and points to consider in directing the discussion.

HOW IT WORKS

The premise of this series is simple: use this book as a kit to use in building your own Bible study on a topic of importance to young people. Sometimes a leader has time to plan out and prepare a Bible study in advance; sometimes we all find ourselves rushing to catch up on responsibilities. This book can be used in both circumstances; a leader can simply select a few questions and activities from each section and use them in studying the passage, or he can use the materials in this book to put together his own questions, activities, and Scripture passages.

Either way, a few things are needed each week from the leader. First, read carefully through the Scripture passage that is provided, and determine what direction the discussion ought to take. Plan some sort of fun activity for an opener; it doesn't need to be complicated, but it should not be thrown together at the very last minute. Finally, and most importantly, pray! Pray that the Lord will teach you the truths from His Word, pray that you will be a good role model in practicing those truths, and pray that He will be at work in the hearts and minds of the young people in your group.

Why Fuzzy Brain?

Fuzzy brain is fuzzy thinking: sort of an unclear picture of what things really look like. We all have some fuzzy ideas about various things; our understanding of quantum physics, for example, may not be as clear as those of a physicist.There are some things in life, however, that are far too important to allow any fuzzy thinking. Someone who is unclear on just what traffic lights mean will not be driving for long.

Issues of life and death are no joking matter, and we all take care to educate our young people on how to live safely. How much more, then, should we be concerned about how our young people view issues of eternal life and death? That is what this book is for. This is a flexible study tool for those who are leading small group Bible studies with young people, around middle- and high-school age. The topic is the gospel, specifically how the teachings of Christ compare with those of world religions.

Theology

However, in dealing with this topic, we will need to have some background understanding of the basics of our world: who are we, how we got here, who is God, what is sin, and so forth. We will avoid technical theological terms such as "justification" or "propitiation" as much as possible, and will address these issues in everyday terms that all can understand.

This is actually a study about the two Adams, the old Adam and the Second Adam. It is a book about being born again into the family of the Second Adam, what that means and how it's done. It is also about why being born again is of eternal importance.

Who It's For

This book is designed for young people who have little or no background on the teachings of Jesus Christ. It is a tool to use in reaching out to the unchurched young people in your neighborhood, those who do not have any clear picture of who Jesus is or what He teaches.

It is also designed for those who have been indoctrinated into the world's way of thinking: that there are many gods and many ways of getting in touch with them. In the course of these seven studies, you will gradually bring your young people to the point of confrontation with Jesus Himself, who demands that we understand that there is one God and one mediator between God and man. "No one comes to the Father except through Me."

STUDY 01

Where'd We Come From?

GENESIS 1

When addressing any topic, one should begin at the beginning. That is exactly what we will do in this study, as we go all the way back to the beginning of time and watch as God creates the entire world.

At first glance, this may not seem to have much to do with Jesus' death and resurrection or with world religions, yet it in fact has everything to do with these topics. In order to understand the differences among religious systems, we must first understand who God is, who we are, and how the world got to be the way it is. This is the foundation for any worldview, any religious system, and any faith in God.

Some in our society teach us that the world came from a "big bang." They are not suggesting that God used a mighty explosion to begin the creation process; they are claiming that there was a random explosion of some sort which began a series of random events known as evolution.

The Bible gives us a very different picture. There is no mention of any bangs, just words. God spoke, and it was. This is a very significant difference; a bang is just an inarticulate noise with no intelligence or meaning behind it. Words require meaning, thought, and a mind with a plan. God's plan was to create a perfect world filled with perfect beings who lived together in perfect happiness.

Let's listen to God as He speaks the world into existence and learn a little about Who He is and what His plans are.

ACTIVITIES

Choose one of the activities below.

CLAY CREATORS. Give each person a lump of clay and a time limit for them each to "create" a work of art. When finished, go around the group and let them describe to the rest of the class their clay creations and why they chose to make them.

THE UNKNOWN ARTIST. Divide the group into pairs, and hand out paper and colored pencils, markers, or crayons. Have each person draw a simple sketch of the other person in their pair. When finished show the sketches to the class and have them guess who the model is for each sketch.

ICEBREAKERS

Choose one or two of these icebreakers.

››› What hobbies do you have? Do you enjoy any creative things, such as music or building things?

››› If you could be any animal, bird, or fish, what would you be? Why?

››› Since you aren't a bird or a fish, why is it better to be human? What would it really be like to be the animal you selected?

SCRIPTURE READING

Read the following passage from Genesis.

READER ONE [1] In the beginning God created the heavens and the earth. [2] Now the earth was formless and empty, darkness was over the surface of the deep, and the Spirit of God was hovering over the waters.

READER TWO [3] And God said, "Let there be light," and there was light. [4] God saw that the light was good, and he separated the light from the darkness. [5] God called the light "day," and the darkness he called "night." And there was evening, and there was morning—the first day.

READER THREE [6] And God said, "Let there be an expanse between the waters to separate water from water." [7] So God made the expanse and separated the water under the expanse from the water above it. And it was so. [8] God called the expanse "sky." And there was evening, and there was morning—the second day.

READER FOUR [9] And God said, "Let the water under the sky be gathered to one place, and let dry ground appear." And it was so. [10] God called the dry ground "land," and the gathered waters he called "seas." And God saw that it was good.

READER ONE [11] Then God said, "Let the land produce vegetation: seed-bearing plants and trees on the land that bear fruit with seed in it, according to their various kinds." And it was so. [12] The land produced vegetation: plants bearing seed according to their kinds and trees bearing fruit with seed in it according to their kinds. And God saw that it was good. [13] And there was evening, and there was morning-the third day.

READER TWO [14] And God said, "Let there be lights in the expanse of the sky to separate the day from the night, and let them serve as signs to mark seasons and days and years, [15] and let them be lights in the expanse of the sky to give light on the earth." And it was so. [16] God made two great lights—the greater light to govern the day and the lesser light to govern the night. He also made the stars. [17] God set them in the expanse of the sky to give light on the earth, [18] to govern the day and the night, and to separate light from darkness. And God saw that it was good.

[19] And there was evening, and there was morning-the fourth day.

READER THREE: [20] And God said, "Let the water teem with living creatures, and let birds fly above the earth across the expanse of the sky." [21] So God created the great creatures of the sea and every living and moving thing with which the water teems, according to their kinds, and every winged bird according to its kind. And God saw that it was good. [22] God blessed them and said, "Be fruitful and increase in number and fill the water in the seas, and let the birds increase on the earth." [23] And there was evening, and there was morning-the fifth day.

READER FOUR: [24] And God said, "Let the land produce living creatures according to their kinds: livestock, creatures that move along the ground, and wild animals, each according to its kind." And it was so. [25] God made the wild animals according to their kinds, the livestock according to their kinds, and all the creatures that move along the ground according to their kinds. And God saw that it was good.

READER ONE: [26] Then God said, "Let us make man in our image, in our likeness, and let them rule over the fish of the sea and the birds of the air, over the livestock, over all the earth, and over all the creatures that move along the ground."

READER TWO: [27] So God created man in his own image, in the image of God he created him; male and female he created them.

READER THREE: [28] God blessed them and said to them, "Be fruitful and increase in number; fill the earth and subdue it. Rule over the fish of the sea and the birds of the air and over every living creature that moves on the ground."

READER FOUR: [29] Then God said, "I give you every seed-bearing plant on the face of the whole earth and every tree that has fruit with seed in it. They will be yours for food. [30] And to all the beasts of the earth and all the birds of the air and all the creatures that move on the ground-everything that has the breath of life in it-I give every green plant for food." And it was so.

READER ONE: [31] God saw all that he had made, and it was very good. And there was evening, and there was morning-the sixth day.

Genesis 1:1-31

DISCUSSION QUESTIONS

Select four to five questions from the head
and heart sections, and/or make up your own.

>>> Note that every paragraph in this story begins with "God." Why
is God mentioned so much?
Notice Wiersbe page 1.

>>> How does God create in this chapter? What tools does He use to
make the heavens and the earth and everything that lives and
grows on the earth?

>>> Does it seem like God is just making it up as He goes along, or
does He seem to have a definite plan in mind?

>>> Why does the writer keep saying "according to their kinds" (v.
11,12,21,24,25)? What does this mean?

>>> What does it mean that, at each stage of creation, "God saw
that it was good"?

>>> What does it mean that God made man in His image? What do
human beings have that makes us like God? What things make
us different from "the fish of the sea and the birds of the air"
and "the livestock" of earth (v. 26)?

Also notice page 2 of Wiersbe paper!

>>> How does modern science explain the earth's origins? How does
modern science explain the origins of the human race?

>>> Which of these accounts—the Bible's and science's—seems eas-
ier to believe in?

>>> What is the major difference between the theories of science
(evolution) and the teachings of the Bible (creation)? Who or
what is missing from science's theories?

>>> How does the Bible's view of mankind (image of God) differ from that of modern science (evolved from apes)? Which view puts a higher value on human life?

>>> Would you prefer to live in a world that evolved by accident, or one that was created by God?

CARING TIME

Use these questions or make up your own.

>>> The Bible teaches that God created everything from nothing; the world around you teaches you that everything just sort of happened by accident. How does it make you feel to discover that the world might be wrong?

>>> If God did create the world as the Bible says, how does that affect your views on life? On yourself?

>>> If God actually created the world just by saying, "Let there be." and there was, how does that affect your view of God?

>>> God looked on His creation and saw that it was good. Do you agree? Why or why not?

NEXT WEEK

This week we went back in time and watched as God created the entire world. In the coming week, pay attention to the world around you—to plants and animals and things that you see—and ask yourself if it could have all happened by accident. Next week we will continue this story to see just where people fit in.

1:1 In the beginning God. These words summarize our purpose in this study. We are discovering that there was a definite beginning to life, and God was the One Who created it. He is everywhere during creation—in the heavens, on the earth, in the sky, under the oceans—creating all from nothing and filling the world with life.

*Notice Wiersbe page about Creator.

1:3 And God said, "Let there be light," and there was light. That's all there is to it. No tools, no sweat, no trial and error—He simply spoke, and it was. The power and wisdom of God are beyond human comprehension. Consider John 1:1-3: "In the beginning was the Word; and the Word was with God, and the Word was God. He was with God in the beginning. All things were created through Him, and apart from Him not one thing was created that has been created." Jesus is the Incarnate Word, the Word Become Flesh. This further demonstrates the completeness of God's plan, the plan that He'd designed before creation.

1:5 the first day. God has a definite plan; He is not making it up as He goes along. Before He can grow plants He must have dry ground, which requires that waters be separated, and so forth. The order of creation is: 1. heavens, earth, light; 2. atmosphere (sky); 3. dry ground, seas, vegetation; 4. sun, moon, stars; 5. fish, birds; 6. livestock, wild animals, land animals, man; 7. rest (Gen. 2:1-3).

1:11 according to their various kinds. There is a basic assumption here that like produces like—that is, that a bird brings forth a bird, not a fish. This seems obvious, yet the teachings of evolution are based upon the assumption that a creature can change its form and its nature, given enough time. If this were so, then mankind would be able to free itself from the bondage of death by evolving into a higher being, having no need of a savior. As we shall see in the coming weeks, this is not so.

1:18 And God saw that it was good. God's creation was good—very good (1:31)—until man sinned. At that point creation was made subject to death, and good was mixed with evil. It is important to recognize, however, that God originally intended that man live in a perfect world, free from suffering, poverty, illness, war, and death. When we ask "Why would a good God make people suffer?" the answer is that He didn't—man did. God's creation was good and perfect at the beginning.

1:22 Be fruitful and increase. God's original purpose for creation was that all His creatures live in happiness and prosperity, reproducing and filling the earth with peaceful, harmonious creatures. Best of all, "God blessed them." People are created to live in peaceful communion with God, seeing His face (as we'll see in the next study) and being abundantly blessed.

1:26 Let us make man in our image. Only people are made in God's image; we are different from all other creatures. To be made in His image means many things, such as our ability to create, which no animal shares. One of the most significant aspects, however, is free will: we have the ability to choose between good and evil. That was the reason that God planted the forbidden tree in the garden, which we will learn of next week, because otherwise the entire earth was all good. Without the presence of something evil, man would have had no choice but to be good. Being in God's image means having free will, being creative, having the ability to reason and think on abstract principles, being able to communicate through language, and many other things. People are unique in creation, and each human being is of incomparable value. **let them rule.** We have been given the responsibility for the care and maintenance of earth. This does not mean that we can enslave or abuse or exploit the earth. It also does not mean that we must never cut down a tree or mine for oil or raise domestic livestock. It means that we must be a good stewards, caring for all of God's creation, because it is good.

1:27 male and female. We are speaking of both male and female humans. Chapter 2 makes it clear that both are needed to complete the image of God on our race. Both are equal before God in this sense; a man without a woman is "not good" (2:18).

20

STUDY 02

Who Am I?

GENESIS 2 AND 3

Last week we watched as God created the heavens and the earth. He made it perfect, free from sin or death, a place of harmony and joy and peace. This week, however, we will watch man's first acts as the new lord of creation.

God gave Adam the job of overseeing and caring for His creation, giving him complete, free rein over everything. He was free to eat from any tree, free to name and oversee the animals, free to tend the garden... free.

With this freedom, however, came a more powerful freedom: the freedom to imagine the possibilities and consequences of action and then choose. God made us with free will, the ability to choose between two or more courses of action. This is different from the rest of earthly creation; the animals and lower life forms choose to act largely based upon instinct and habit. We choose our own course with thoughtful reason.

This free will, of course, would have been meaningless if there were not different options to choose from, so God also planted a tree in the middle of the garden known as the tree of the knowledge of good and evil. This tree, God said, would bring death, so Adam was not to eat from it. It was the only restriction; everything else was good and acceptable. Adam had the freedom to choose to obey God, which raised him from the level of slave or robot to one of friend. God will not force anyone to love Him, and love freely given will be demonstrated by obedience.

These concepts will be important to understand as we proceed in these studies. We must understand that we deliberately chose to serve sin and death if we are to understand the justice and grace of God in freeing us from that curse.

ACTIVITIES

Choose one of the activities below.

TWO TRUTHS AND A LIE Go around the circle and have each person tell the group three things about themselves—two being true, and one being a lie. They must tell them in random order, and it should be difficult to know which are true and which one is false. The group must guess which thing is the lie.

FRUIT-BASKET TURNOVER Have the group sit in a circle, with one person standing in the middle and all the chairs filled. Each person, including the person in the middle, must go around the circle and call out the name of a different fruit. The person in the middle then calls out two fruits—"banana and cherry"—and those two fruits must get up and exchange seats while the person in the middle tries to grab the empty chair. The person in the middle can also call out "fruit-basket turnover" and everyone must get up and find a new seat. Whoever does not have a seat after each round then calls out two new fruits, etc.

ICEBREAKERS

Choose one or two of these icebreakers.

›› What's the craziest outfit you've ever worn?

›› What's your favorite fruit?

›› If you could know anything, what one thing would you most like to know?

SCRIPTURE READING

Read the following passages from Genesis 2 and 3.

Genesis 2

READER ONE ¹⁵ The LORD God took the man and put him in the Garden of Eden to work it and take care of it. ¹⁶ And the LORD God commanded the man, "You are free to eat from any tree in the garden; ¹⁷ but you must not eat from the tree of the knowledge of good and evil, for when you eat of it you will surely die."

Genesis 3

READER TWO ¹ Now the serpent was more crafty than any of the wild animals the LORD God had made. He said to the woman, "Did God really say, 'You must not eat from any tree in the garden'?" ² The woman said to the serpent, "We may eat fruit from the trees in the garden, ³ but God did say, 'You must not eat fruit from the tree that is in the middle of the garden, and you must not touch it, or you will die.' "

READER THREE ⁴ "You will not surely die," the serpent said to the woman. ⁵ "For God knows that when you eat of it your eyes will be opened, and you will be like God, knowing good and evil."

READER FOUR ⁶ When the woman saw that the fruit of the tree was good for food and pleasing to the eye, and also desirable for gaining wisdom, she took some and ate it. She also gave some to her husband, who was with her, and he ate it. ⁷ Then the eyes of both of them were opened, and they realized they were naked; so they sewed fig leaves together and made coverings for themselves.

READER FIVE ⁸ Then the man and his wife heard the sound of the LORD God as he was walking in the garden in the cool of the day, and they hid from the LORD God among the trees of the garden. ⁹ But the LORD God called to the man, "Where are you?" ¹⁰ He answered, "I heard you in the garden, and I was afraid because I was naked; so I hid."

READER ONE: [11] And he said, "Who told you that you were naked? Have you eaten from the tree that I commanded you not to eat from?" [12] The man said, "The woman you put here with me-she gave me some fruit from the tree, and I ate it."

READER TWO: [13] Then the LORD God said to the woman, "What is this you have done?" The woman said, "The serpent deceived me, and I ate." [14] So the LORD God said to the serpent, "Because you have done this, Cursed are you above all the livestock and all the wild animals! You will crawl on your belly and you will eat dust all the days of your life. [15] And I will put enmity between you and the woman, and between your offspring and hers; he will crush your head, and you will strike his heel."

READER THREE: [16] To the woman he said, "I will greatly increase your pains in childbearing; with pain you will give birth to children. Your desire will be for your husband, and he will rule over you."

READER FOUR: [17] To Adam he said, "Because you listened to your wife and ate from the tree about which I commanded you, 'You must not eat of it,' Cursed is the ground because of you; through painful toil you will eat of it all the days of your life. [18] It will produce thorns and thistles for you, and you will eat the plants of the field. [19] By the sweat of your brow you will eat your food until you return to the ground, since from it you were taken; for dust you are and to dust you will return."

READER FIVE: [20] Adam named his wife Eve, because she would become the mother of all the living. [21] The LORD God made garments of skin for Adam and his wife and clothed them. [22] And the LORD God said, "The man has now become like one of us, knowing good and evil. He must not be allowed to reach out his hand and take also from the tree of life and eat, and live forever." [23] So the LORD God banished him from the Garden of Eden to work the ground from which he had been taken. [24] After he drove the man out, he placed on the east side of the Garden of Eden cherubim and a flaming sword flashing back and forth to guard the way to the tree of life.

Genesis 2:15-17; 3:1-24

DISCUSSION QUESTIONS

Select four or five questions from the head and heart sections, and/or make up your own.

>>> Why does God tell Adam that he is "free" (2:16)? How can he be free if there is something he is told not to do (2:17)?

>>> What is "the knowledge of good and evil" (2:17)? Why does it cause death?

>>> How does the serpent deceive Eve? What lies does he tell her?

>>> Why did Eve eat the forbidden fruit? Why did Adam? Why did the serpent tell Eve to eat it in the first place?

>>> Why do Adam and Eve hide from God (3:8)? Why does God ask them questions? Does He not know already?

>>> What was life like on earth before Adam ate the fruit? What was it like after?

>>> How did God originally intend for life on earth to be? How is life different from what God intended?

>>> Why did God forbid Adam to eat the fruit "of the knowledge of good and evil"?

>>> Why does this knowledge bring death? If it is so deadly, why did God put it there?

>>> What does it mean that there will be "enmity" between the serpent and the descendants of Adam and Eve (3:15)? What does it mean that Eve will bear children in pain (3:16)? That Adam will eat food "by the sweat of your brow" (3:19)?

>>> How does this history explain the suffering and death that is in the world today?

CARING TIME

Use these questions or make up your own.

Conclude the meeting with prayer. Make sure that the issues raised by the group are submitted to God.

>>> The Bible teaches us that this story really happened, that Adam and Eve were real people—that this is not a mere myth. Is it important that you believe this?

>>> God intended men to live in peace and happiness. Whose fault is it that we now have wars and sorrow?

>>> God came looking for Adam and Eve after they sinned, even though they were hiding. What does that tell you about God? About mankind?

NEXT WEEK

This week we witnessed the fall of humans, as the very first man that was ever alive chose deliberately to sin against God, knowing all the while that he would be bringing death into the world. In the coming week, pay attention to the news and ask yourself how much of the world's suffering is the fault of human beings. Next week will consider the concept of sin.

2:15 you are free. Only mankind was given the freedom to make reasoned choices; God did not give this freedom to any of the animals. Presumably, they merely ate what instinct told them to eat, whereas man was free to experiment and taste and learn.

2:17 you must not eat. This is God's first commandment and was originally the only law humans needed. It is comparable to telling a child, "You must not play with matches, for when you do you will surely be burned." It was, a fatherly warning, motivated not by a desire to restrict or forbid or oppress, but to protect. **tree of the knowledge of good and evil.** It may seem as though any lack of knowledge is a lack of power and enrichment, but in reality some forms of "knowing" are evil and destructive. The term "to know" indicates an intimate understanding and communion. (The King James Bible uses the word when it speaks of sexual union.) God wants men and women to have an intimate understanding and communion with Himself—but He wants it to be voluntary. He gives us a choice. **you will surely die.** Death was not part of God's will for people. He told Adam not to know death. Again, this was not a stern heavy-handed threat that He would violently punish the smallest disobedience; it was an up-front warning that eating that particular fruit would bring death. Disobeying God's commands always causes us to be separated from Him, which is death.

3:1 the serpent. The Bible informs us elsewhere that the serpent is the Devil—Satan, who had been an angel but had rebelled against God. He was thrown out of heaven, and his angels went with him. The Devil and his demonic followers are real, and they hate people because we are like (in the image of) God. He cannot harm God, so he tries to harm us instead. **"Did God really say...?"** Satan's first recorded words to humans are to question God's Word. He is still at it today, questioning the authority of God's Word as it is revealed in Scripture and in the person of Jesus Christ. **any tree.** Of course, God had not said this. In fact, God had told Adam, "You are free to eat." Satan's next tactic was to falsely accuse God of saying something mean or restrictive.

3:2 The woman said to the serpent. Perhaps Eve would have done better to flee rather than to discuss, but she may have been ignorant of who the serpent was. At any rate, we now know who the Devil is, and we must flee his lies and temptations, not try to argue or rationalize or debate.

3:3 you must not touch it. God did not say that. Eve actually helps the Devil when she adds to God's Word.

3:4 "You will not surely die." The first lie. Satan is "the father of lies," and from the very beginning people have believed them. His lie has not changed; the world today continues to believe that we can do as we please without consequences, and the world also continues to reject God's Word.

3:5 For God knows. Satan next accuses God of evil motives. "He just doesn't want you to be wise, he wants to keep you down, to oppress you. He knows that if you eat that fruit you'll be equal to Him, and then He'd lose His power over you. Eat and be liberated!" We still hear this lie today in many forms, but Satan's "liberation" still ends in death and despair.

3:6 When the woman saw. Eve was deceived. Satan had tricked her, and she relied on her own eyes and her own wisdom rather than on the free will that she'd been given to obey. Perhaps she believed that by eating she was somehow obeying God. Regardless, it is no coincidence that Satan chose to tempt the woman. **gave some to her husband.** Adam was not deceived. He knew that he was disobeying God, yet he chose to eat just the same. We are not told why he ate, but the important fact is that he chose to do so. The operative words here are "he chose." They voluntarily, knowingly, and deliberately chose to sin and to bring death and evil into the world. The New Testament, as we shall see, tells us that it was Adam's sin, not Eve's, which brought death; it was his deliberate choice of whom to obey.

3:7 made coverings. We are told in 2:25 that Adam and Eve were naked yet knew no shame. The very first thing to happen when they gained the knowledge of evil was to know shame. The first thing in creation to experience death was the relationship between man and woman, as they both tried to hide their nakedness.

3:8 as he was walking. Perhaps God often came and walked with Adam and Eve, talking with them face to face. Unfortunately, this came to an end on that day, and the next relationship to "die" was between man and God: "they hid from the LORD God."

3:9 But the LORD God called to the man. Immediately God set about working to restore the lost relationship. God has wanted reconciliation with Adam and all people from the beginning, and it has always been God who initiates it. God asked questions of Adam to lead him to confess his sin, for without confession of sin there can be no salvation. God was not asking for information; He already knew. He was immediately working toward our redemption.

3:12 The woman you put here. "It's the woman's fault—she gave me the fruit. No, wait—it's your fault because You put her here with me. It can't be my fault!" Note that free will includes the freedom to hide, deny, and blame others. Yet, at least Adam chose to answer God when He called (3:10); he could have chosen not to. Answering God's call is the first step in reconciliation and salvation.

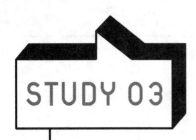

STUDY 03

Sin? What's That All About?

ROMANS 3; 5; AND 6

Last week we saw where sin comes from: Adam deliberately disobeyed what God told him to do. But that was Adam! He lived a long time ago. What does his problem have to do with us? In this week's study we will learn that Adam's sin brought death into the world. It was a sort of agreement that he had with God: eat good fruit and prosper; eat the forbidden fruit and die. Adam knew this up front, yet he decided voluntarily to embrace death.

There are two basic concepts at work in this study: God's justice, and our sinful nature. God's justice demands that He keep His word: if you sin, you will die. Human nature is sinful from the womb, as we will see in more detail in future studies. Adam and Eve could not give birth to sinless people, because they themselves were not sinless people. A bird, after all, cannot bring forth a baby snail.

Sin is falling short of the glory of God. This means that a person has not been perfect. What an impossible standard! Who can live up to perfection? The very fact that we instinctively ask that question demonstrates that all people know they are not perfect. All must recognize that they are sinners and have fallen short of God's commands.

God is just in allowing people to live in a world of death, because each one of us has voluntarily chosen to do so. Each person has voluntarily chosen to sin simply because it is our nature to do so; we are all descendants of Adam.

ACTIVITIES

Choose one of the activities below.

>>> X Marks the Spot—put an "x" of tape on a wall and have each member of the group take a turn in throwing a soft ball at the "x", seeing who can come the closest. Set a designated throwing line that will make it difficult to hit the mark.

>>> Hoop Toss—mark a large circle with tape, put everyone outside the circle with one blindfolded person in the middle. The blindfolded member has to throw a softball into a basket with only the verbal directions of those outside the circle.

ICEBREAKERS

Choose one or two of these icebreakers.

>>> What was the most exciting gift you ever received? What was the most costly you ever gave?

>>> Where were you born?

>>> Has someone ever proven that they love you in some drastic way? Or have you done that for someone else? Tell the group about it.

SCRIPTURE READING

Read the following passages from Romans.

Romans 3

`READER ONE` [5] ...Is God unrighteous to inflict wrath? [6] Absolutely not! Otherwise, how will God judge the world?

[9] There is no one righteous, not even one;
[11] there is no one who understands, there is no one who seeks God.
[12] All have turned away, together they have become useless;
   there is no one who does good, there is not even one.

[23] For all have sinned and fall short of the glory of God.

Romans 5

`READER TWO` [6] For while we were still helpless, at the appointed moment, Christ died for the ungodly. [8] But God proves His own love for us in that while we were still sinners Christ died for us! [12] Therefore, just as sin entered the world through one man, and death through sin, in this way death spread to all men, because all sinned.

`READER THREE` [15] But the gift is not like the trespass. For if by the one man's trespass the many died, how much more have the grace of God and the gift overflowed to the many by the grace of the one man, Jesus Christ. [16] And the gift is not like the one man's sin, because from one sin came the judgment, resulting in condemnation, but from many trespasses came the gift, resulting in justification. [17] Since by the one man's trespass, death reigned through that one man, how much more will those who receive the overflow of grace and the gift of righteousness reign in life through the one man, Jesus Christ.

`READER FOUR` [18] So then, as through one trespass there is condemnation for everyone, so also through one righteous act there is life-giving justification for everyone. [19] For just as through one man's disobedience the many were made sinners, so also through the one man's obedience the many will be made righteous.

Romans 6

²³ For the wages of sin is death, but the gift of God is eternal life in Christ Jesus our Lord.

Romans 3:5,6,9-12,23; 5:6,8,12,15-19; 6:23

DISCUSSION QUESTIONS

Select four or five questions from the head and heart sections, and/or make up your own.

››› What does Paul mean that "sin entered the world through one man" (5:12)?

››› Why did "death spread to all men" (5:12)?

››› Why have all people ("the many") become sinners "through one man's disobedience" (5:19)? Why can't people live sinless lives?

››› Why is there "condemnation for everyone" (5:18)? Why is God angry?

››› What is the difference between "wages" and a "gift" (6:23)? Why is death the paycheck of sin?

››› If death is the paycheck for sin, does that mean that mankind has earned death?

››› What hope did mankind have of ever escaping from sin and death? What hope do we have now?

››› What is "the gift" that Paul is speaking of in these verses?

››› Who is the "one man" whose disobedience made all people ("the many") sinners (5:19)? ~~Why is it that we have all been born with sinful natures?~~

>>> Who is the "one man" whose obedience will make people righteous—that is, forgiven for sin (5:19)? ~~What was His "obedience"?~~

>>> If eternal life is a gift from God, how does a person get it? What motivates God to offer the gift (5:8)?

CARING TIME

Use these questions or make up your own.

Close in group prayer, being mindful that some may be drawn to God. Be prepared to explain the way of salvation.

>>> The Bible tells us that we have all sinned. What kinds of sins are common to people? Do you struggle with any of these common sins?

>>> How can the sins common to all people bring death?

>>> Do you understand that being "born again" through Christ—the Second Adam—brings eternal life? How does that solve the problem with sin?

>>> Have you accepted God's free gift of eternal life? If not, would you like to right now?

NEXT WEEK

This week we learned that every human who has ever lived has sinned. We are all unable to avoid sin simply because we are descended from Adam. But we also have discovered that God has offered a free gift to anyone who wants it. In the coming week, pray that God would give you that gift and teach you more about who He is. Next week we will learn that there was one Man who lived a life without sinning, a man who was both human and divine.

3:5–6 Is God unrighteous to inflict wrath? God is proven righteous when He keeps His word. He warned Adam that sin would bring death. This is God's justice: the absolutely fair enforcement of righteousness which brings both judgment for the unrighteous and reward for the righteous. Unfortunately, as we are told in verse 9, there aren't any who are righteous. This will lead us, in a future study, to God's grace, but for now we must first understand God's justice.

3:9–12 no one righteous. As we have already seen in Genesis, like brings forth like; fish produce fish, birds produce birds, and sinners produce sinners. Adam's children were born with Adam's sinful nature, and there is no one who has ever been born since who did not share in Adam's nature. A bird cannot become a tiger, and a sinner cannot evolve into a sinless being. There is (thus far) no hope for us to ever become righteous simply because we are born from the sinful Adam. What we need is a second Adam, founder of a new "race," in order that we might be "born again" into a new nature that is without sin. If we realize how utterly hopeless and impossible this is, we may become filled with joy when we discover that it is really true.

5:6 Christ died for the ungodly. The overwhelming truth is that Jesus became that Second Adam, through whom we have redemption from our sinful nature. We will study this more fully as we go along, but for now Paul lets us know that we should not despair: God has made a way!

5:12 through one man. Here again Paul reminds us that Adam chose death over life. Some may argue that God was harsh to condemn the entire race to death because Adam and Eve ate some fruit. But the opposite is true: obedience was so very easy for Adam—he had to go out of his way to commit sin. His act of eating from the forbidden tree was actually a deliberate, conscious choice to disobey God. He was knowingly choosing, with his free will, to bring death into the world. God has been perfectly just in allowing Adam and his descendants to have the death which was chosen.

5:15 the gift is not like the trespass. This section may be hard for young people to understand. Paul is comparing God's justice with God's grace, which we will study more later. Basically, death is our due, our wage—we have earned it, it is ours by right and by birth. Life (and justification and righteousness) are a gift, something that is not ours by right, something which we have not earned. This again is the difference between our paycheck from last week and an unexpected gift.

6:23 wages ... gift. Once more Paul emphasizes this theme: death is our wage, we have earned it. It is our birth-right, our heritage—we are descendants of Adam, which means that we have inherited Adam's nature by simply being born. To some this may sound unfair, but it is actually perfectly just: it is God faithfully keeping the promise He made to Adam. We often clamor for justice and fairness, but in truth God's perfect justice condemns us all, for we all have sinned. When we come to understand this fact, we realize how hopeless the human condition is, and we marvel at the miraculous gift of God's grace through Jesus Christ, the Second Adam.

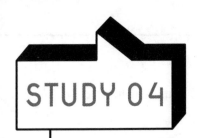

STUDY 04

Okay, So Who's This God?

MATTHEW 9:16:20:27 AND 28

We have learned about the world and how it was created, about man and his sinful condition, and about the justice of God which allows man to continue in sin and death. This week we must look more at the Person of God to understand more fully just who He is.

The justice of God is just one of His holy attributes. This week we will balance that with a first look at His grace, the grace which sent a Redeemer to earth. This Redeemer is a man, born from a human woman, yet He is also God, born not through a human father. This man's Father is God Himself, and this man bears a dual nature: fully God and fully human.

Jesus calls Himself "the Son of Man" repeatedly in the gospels, and today we will look at a few of those passages. This is a title which may sound odd to modern American ears, but to Jesus' contemporaries it carried a message: the Son of Man would be the Messiah.

This study will help young people to begin recognizing the key differences between Christianity and various world religious systems. There are no other religions established that feature a man who is both God and human. There are no other religions that have been founded by a man who rose again from the dead.

The resurrection is central to Christian belief, because it proves that Jesus has won victory over death. He has, by voluntarily giving up a sinless life (not subject to death Himself), satisfied once and for all the justice of God, and He has brought into the world the endless bounties of God's grace.

ACTIVITIES

Choose one of the activities below.

FREEZE TAG If the meeting place permits, set up a short game of freeze tag with one person as "it." Once tagged by "it," another player must come and tag you again to "unfreeze" you.

BLIND TRUST Set up an obstacle course in a large room and divide the group into teams for a blind race. One member of each team is allowed to go into the room and see the course. Then one at a time a blindfolded team member from each team is brought in. The sighted member must guide the blind member by voice command through the course. Once that member completes the course he brings in the next member blindfolded and the two sighted members must talk the blinded member through the course. Each time the member who has just completed the course helps with verbal commands. Both teams do this simultaneously until one team has all of its member through the course.

ICEBREAKERS

Choose one or two of these icebreakers.

››› Have you ever been confused about someone's identity, mistaking a stranger for someone you knew, etc.? What happened? Why were you confused? How did you discover the truth?

››› If you could have the attributes of one animal, while still being a human, what animal would you choose?

››› When have you been almost defeated (in sports, school, or other competition) then suddenly burst ahead to victory?

SCRIPTURE READING

Read the following passages from Matthew.

Matthew 9

`READER ONE:` ¹So Jesus got into a boat, crossed over, and came to His own town. ² Just then some men brought to Him a paralytic lying on a stretcher. Seeing their faith, Jesus told the paralytic, "Have courage, son, your sins are forgiven." ³ At this, some of the scribes said among themselves, "He's blaspheming!" ⁴ But perceiving their thoughts, Jesus said, "Why are you thinking evil things in your hearts? ⁵ For which is easier: to say, 'Your sins are forgiven,' or to say, 'Get up and walk'? ⁶ But so you may know that the Son of Man has authority on earth to forgive sins"—then He told the paralytic, "Get up, pick up your stretcher, and go home." ⁷ And he got up and went home.

Matthew 16

`READER TWO:` ¹³ When Jesus came to the region of Caesarea Philippi, He asked His disciples, "Who do people say that the Son of Man is?" ¹⁴ And they said, "Some say John the Baptist; others, Elijah; still others, Jeremiah or one of the prophets." ¹⁵ "But you," He asked them, "who do you say that I am?" ¹⁶ Simon Peter answered, "You are the Messiah, the Son of the living God!" ¹⁷ And Jesus responded, "Blessed are you, Simon son of Jonah, because flesh and blood did not reveal this to you, but My Father in heaven.

Matthew 20

`READER THREE:` ¹⁷ While going up to Jerusalem, Jesus took the 12 disciples aside privately and said to them on the way: ¹⁸ "Listen! We are going up to Jerusalem. The Son of Man will be handed over to the chief priests and scribes, and they will condemn Him to death. ¹⁹ Then they will hand Him over to the Gentiles to be mocked, flogged, and crucified, and He will be resurrected on the third day."

Matthew 27   ³⁵ After crucifying Him they divided His clothes by casting lots. ³⁷ Above His head they put up the charge against Him in writing:

THIS IS JESUS
THE KING OF THE JEWS

³⁸ Then two criminals were crucified with Him, one on the right and one on the left. ³⁹ Those who passed by were yelling insults at Him, shaking their heads ⁴⁰ and saying, ... "If You are the Son of God, come down from the cross!" ⁴¹ In the same way the chief priests, with the scribes and elders, mocked Him and said, ⁴² "He saved others, but He cannot save Himself! ⁴³ ... For He said, 'I am God's Son.' "

Matthew 28

READER FOUR. ¹After the Sabbath, as the first day of the week was dawning, Mary Magdalene and the other Mary went to view the tomb. ² Suddenly there was a violent earthquake, because an angel of the Lord descended from heaven and approached the tomb. He rolled back the stone and was sitting on it. ³ His appearance was like lightning, and his robe was as white as snow. ⁴ The guards were so shaken from fear of him that they became like dead men.
⁵ But the angel told the women, "Don't be afraid, because I know you are looking for Jesus who was crucified. ⁶ He is not here! For He has been resurrected, just as He said. Come and see the place where He lay. ⁷ Then go quickly and tell His disciples, 'He has been raised from the dead. In fact, He is going ahead of you to Galilee; you will see Him there.' Listen, I have told you."
⁸ So, departing quickly from the tomb with fear and great joy, they ran to tell His disciples the news. ⁹ Just then Jesus met them and said, "Rejoice!" They came up, took hold of His feet, and worshiped Him. ¹⁰ Then Jesus told them, "Do not be afraid. Go and tell My brothers to leave for Galilee, and they will see Me there."

Matthew 9:1-7; 16:13-17; 20:17-19; 27:35,37-42; 28:1-10

DISCUSSION QUESTIONS

Select four or five questions from the head
and heart sections, and/or make up your own.

››› Why does Jesus refer to Himself as "the Son of Man"? How can He be both the Son of Man and the Son of God?

››› Why do the scribes accuse Jesus of blaspheming (9:3)?

››› Why is it important that Jesus' disciples understand who He is (16:13–17)? Why were people in general confused about Him?

››› If Jesus knew in advance that He would be crucified, why did He allow it to happen? Why did He voluntarily die on the cross?

››› Why did Jesus rise again from the dead? What does this prove?

››› Did Jesus forgive the sins of the paralytic man or just heal him? Why is the forgiveness of sins such an important issue in this passage?

››› Are people today still confused about who Jesus is? Who do you say He is?

››› Did Jesus deserve to die? If not, why would a just God allow it to happen?

››› Why did the disciples worship Jesus (28:9)?

››› Why did God become a man? How is He different from Adam?

41

CARING TIME

Use these questions or make up your own.

Close with group prayer remembering the specific questions the group has raised?

>>> Do you believe that Jesus is the Son of God? If not, why? If so, how will that affect your life?

>>> Can Jesus forgive everyone's sins? Can He forgive your sins?

>>> Jesus rose from the grave. What does this mean for you?

>>> What question would you like to submit to God in prayer?

NEXT WEEK

This week we met Jesus, and learned that He is both God and man. In the coming week, pray that God will help you to understand more of who Jesus is, and that He will teach you how to become a follower of Christ. Next week we will learn more about who Jesus is: He is also called the Second Adam.

NOTES ON MATTHEW 9:1-7; 16:13-17; 20:17-19; 27:35, 37-42; 28:1-10

9:3 blasphemy. Who can forgive sins but God alone? The scribes were correct to take issue with Jesus' statement. If He was just a good man, then He has no authority to forgive anyone's sins. A person cannot forgive a crime not done to that person. Only the offended party can forgive. All sin is against God, so God alone can forgive. This is a very important concept to understand, for we must be confronted with the truth of Jesus' true nature: He is God. This was the reason He was crucified, not for healing but for saying He was God.

9:4 evil things in your hearts. The scribes were committing evil, not by recognizing that only God can forgive sin, but by rejecting Jesus' deity despite His actions that proved it. Jesus raised the dead, which only God can do, yet still the scribes and Pharisees reject Him. It is a serious thing to learn of Jesus' sacrifice and to reject it.

9:6 Son of Man. This is the phrase that Jesus used to describe Himself. He was letting His disciples know that He was the Messiah, the Second Adam, who came from God to restore mankind to peace with God, to the position that the first Adam had before he sinned. This can be a difficult concept to grasp, but Jesus is both God and man. It will become more clear in our next study, but for now we should recognize that God Himself became a man in order to deliver us from death.

16:13 Who do people say. It is understandable that people were confused about Jesus' true identity. Never before had God become man. The words Jesus used are also harder for us to understand today, such as "Son of Man" (though they would have been clear to His contemporaries). Our culture likes to say that He was just a powerful teacher, a good man who taught us to be nice to each other. Jesus did not permit this misunderstanding; He confronted His disciples to be sure that they understood clearly that He was the Son of God.

16:17 flesh and blood did not reveal this to you. The truth of God is incomprehensible to man; we need God Himself to reveal truth to us. This is because we have the nature of Adam, which cannot comprehend the nature of God. What we need is a new nature; we need to be born again into a New Adam's race.

20:17–19 they will condemn Him to death. Jesus knew that He was going to be crucified. Even worse, He knew that He would be separated from God. Why did He do this? Jesus took on Himself the sin of mankind, and He bore the rejection from God which is our natural heritage, not His. He died voluntarily because He knew that there was no other way for us to be reconciled to God.

27:39 you are the Son of God. Everyone understood Jesus' claims, from the lowest criminal to the highest ruler. Some believed and others did not, but all knew. That is our job in this study, to ensure that all know the claims of Jesus Christ. Some will believe Him and be saved, while others will reject Him and speak against God; but no one should think that He just taught men to be kind to one another.

28:6 He has been resurrected. The resurrection is of supreme importance, because it proves that Jesus has power over death. This will become clearer in our next study, but for now we must see that Jesus defeated death. If He'd been just a good man, He would still be in the tomb. But when He died, a sinless man, He satisfied God's justice and paid the debt for Adam's sin. In so doing, he broke the bondage of death, bursting out of the grave and setting its captives free.

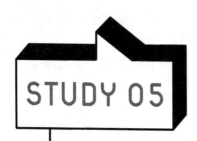

STUDY 05

Death—End of Story?

1 CORINTHIANS 15; ROMANS 6 AND 8

Thus far in this study we have been theoretical, learning about things that happened long ago and coming to understand some very important truths about God and man. But now you are probably asking: "What about me? Where do I fit into all this?"

Beginning with this lesson, we will bring the gospel of Jesus Christ to the personal level, asking ourselves the vital question, "So what will I do with Jesus?" The purpose of our study is to challenge young people to have a personal relationship with Jesus Christ.

In this study we will also consider Jesus as the Second Adam. This means simply that He came to do what Adam failed to do, and in doing so provides us with the opportunity to be born again into a new race. Adam transmits to all of us a sinful nature, under the authority of death. By being born again to the Second Adam, we inherit a new nature and eternal life, freed at last from the bondage of the grave. Just as we now share in Adam's death, so also we will one day share in Jesus' resurrection.

God's justice demands atonement for Adam's sin, an atonement of blood. The Old Testament required God's people to sacrifice lambs to atone for their sins. And this blood cannot be tainted; it must be the blood of a lamb that has no blemish. The requirement is for perfection or sinlessness. Obviously, lambs cannot sin and therefore cannot pay any debt. What is needed is a Lamb that is human.

This is a problem, because no one can live a sinless life. Everyone is bound by the Adamic nature, the nature of sin. Paul refers to this as having the image of Adam. What is needed is someone who is not born of Adam, a person who has a sinless nature, the nature of God. It is for this reason that God, the Son, became human, in order to provide the spotless Lamb to be sacrificed for our sin.

If the concept of the Second Adam is too difficult for your group, focus instead on the fact that Jesus' death has paid the debt for our sin, setting us forever free from sin and death.

ACTIVITIES

Choose one of the activities below.

SEAT OF HONOR Have four or more strong backs pickup a chosen person seated in a substantial dining or desk chair almost to the ceiling. Be careful but not gentle. It is helpful to have energetic music playing while this is done. Repeat this for a number of the group members.

FALLING FOR YOU Have a blindfolded person step up on a table or box and fall backwards into the arms of the group. For added effect have music playing and the lights low. After catching the person raise him or her horizontally chest high and rock this person back and forth with the music.

ICEBREAKERS

Choose one or two of these icebreakers.

>>> What is the most satisfying victory you've ever had? The most disappointing defeat?

>>> What is your favorite room in your house, and why?

>>> If you could become someone else, who would you want to be?

SCRIPTURE READING

Read the following passages from the New Testament.

1 Corinthians 15

READER ONE ¹ Now brothers, I want to clarify for you the gospel I proclaimed to you... that Christ died for our sins according to the Scriptures,
⁴ that He was buried, that He was raised on the third day according to the Scriptures....
²¹ For since death came through a man, the resurrection of the dead also comes through a man. ²² For just as in Adam all die, so also in Christ all will be made alive. ²⁶ The last enemy He abolishes is death. ⁴⁵ So it is written: The first man Adam became a living being; the last Adam became a life-giving Spirit.

READER TWO ⁴⁷ The first man was from the earth and made of dust; the second man is from heaven.
⁴⁸ Like the man made of dust, so are those who are made of dust; like the heavenly man, so are those who are heavenly.
⁴⁹ And just as we have borne the image of the man made of dust, we will also bear the image of the heavenly man.
⁵⁰ Brothers, I tell you this: flesh and blood cannot inherit the kingdom of God, and corruption cannot inherit incorruption.

⁵⁴ Death has been swallowed up in victory.
⁵⁵ O Death, where is your victory?
O Death, where is your sting?
⁵⁶ Now the sting of death is sin, and the power of sin is the law.
⁵⁷ But thanks be to God, who gives us the victory through our Lord Jesus Christ!

Romans 6

READER THREE ³ Or are you unaware that all of us who were baptized into Christ Jesus were baptized into His death? ⁴ Therefore we were buried with Him by baptism into death, in order that, just as Christ was raised from the dead by the glory of the Father, so we too may walk in a new way of life. ⁵ For if we have been joined with Him in the likeness of His death, we will certainly also be in the likeness of His resurrection. ⁶ For we know that our old self was crucified with Him in order that sin's dominion over the body may be abolished, so that we may no longer be enslaved to sin, [7] since a person who has died is freed from sin's claims. [8] Now if we died with Christ, we believe that we will also live with Him, [9] because we know that Christ, having been raised from the dead, no longer dies. Death no longer rules over Him. [10] For in that He died, He died to sin once for all; but in that He lives, He lives to God. [11] So, you too consider yourselves dead to sin, but alive to God in Christ Jesus.

Roman 8

READER FOUR. Therefore, no condemnation now exists for those in Christ Jesus, [2] because the Spirit's law of life in Christ Jesus has set you free from the law of sin and of death. [3] What the law could not do since it was limited by the flesh, God did. He condemned sin in the flesh by sending His own Son in flesh like ours under sin's domain, and as a sin offering, [4] in order that the law's requirement would be accomplished in us who do not walk according to the flesh but according to the Spirit.

[28] We know that all things work together for the good of those who love God: those who are called according to His purpose. [29] For those He foreknew He also predestined to be conformed to the image of His Son, so that He would be the firstborn among many brothers. [30] And those He predestined, He also called; and those He called, He also justified; and those He justified, He also glorified.

READER FIVE. [31] What then are we to say about these things?
If God is for us, who is against us?
[32] He did not even spare His own Son,but offered Him up for us all;
how will He not also with Him grant us everything?
[33] Who can bring an accusation against God's elect?
God is the One who justifies.
[34] Who is the one who condemns?
Christ Jesus is the One who died, but even more, has been raised;
He also is at the right hand of God and intercedes for us.

1 Corinthians 15:1,3-4,21,22,26,45,47-57; Romans 6:3-11; 8:1-4,28-34

DISCUSSION QUESTIONS

Select four or five questions from the head and heart sections, and/or make up your own.

›› How did death come to mankind through a man (1 Cor. 15:21)?

›› What does it mean that Jesus is the Second Adam ("last Adam," 1 Cor. 15:45)?

›› What does it mean to be "baptized into Jesus' death" (Rom. 6:3)? What effect does Jesus' death have for you?

›› What does it mean to "be in the likeness of Jesus' resurrection" (Rom. 6:5)?

›› What is the "law's requirement" (Rom. 8:4)? Why are humans bound to die by this requirement? How did Jesus' death free people from that?

›› Why is it that only a man "from heaven" (1 Cor. 15:47) could defeat death (1 Cor. 15:50)?

›› What does it mean to be "dead to sin" (Rom. 6:11)?

›› What does it mean that Jesus is "the firstborn among many brothers" (Rom. 8:29)? Who are those brothers?

›› How does a person become a brother or sister of Jesus? What exactly happens when a person is born again into Jesus' family?

›› We are all descendant of Adam, who was "made of dust" (1 Cor. 15:47). What does it mean that we bear his image?

›› Jesus is the Second Adam, "from heaven" (1 Cor. 15:47). What would it mean for a person to bear His image?

49

CARING TIME

Use these questions or make up your own.

During your closing prayer you may have to offer some clarification if any of the members had confused answers to these questions.

>>> What do you think it means to be born again into Jesus' family?

>>> How has Jesus defeated sin and death?

>>> Have you been born again into the family of Jesus? If not, would you like to have eternal life?

NEXT WEEK

This week we discovered exactly why God had to become a man in order to free us from death: no one can ever overcome the sinful nature without God's intervention. In the coming week, pray that God would give you the "image of Jesus," saving you from your sinful nature and giving you eternal life. Next week we will compare how the teachings of Jesus differ from all other religions.

NOTES ON 1 CORINTHIANS 15:1,3-4,21,22,26,45,47-57; ROMANS 6:3-11; 8:1-4,28-34

1 Corinthians
15:21 death came through Adam. Adam brought death into the world through his disobedience. Jesus brought "the resurrection of the dead" through His obedience. Adam sinned and was condemned to die. Jesus never sinned and was therefore not condemned to die—He was not subject to death because He was sinless. However, He chose to die in payment for our sins, and in so doing became the Second Adam. To be born again, therefore, means to allow the fleshly nature—the old Adam—to die and to become a child of Christ rather than a child of Adam. Thus, "the last Adam became a life-giving Spirit" (15:45).

15:47 the second man is from heaven. Nobody who has descended from Adam can ever be without sin, because sinners can only give birth to sinners. This is why Jesus was born through a virgin; God is His Father. He was a man, made of human flesh from Mary, but He is also God, not descended from Adam. This is what Paul means when he says that Jesus ("the second man") is from heaven.

15:49 we will also bear the image of the heavenly man. We all bear the image of Adam. We are all sinners; we will all die. Those who are born again will bear the image of the Second Adam: we will be set free from sin and death.

15:50 corruption cannot inherit incorruption. Corruption is death: is of this world and temporary. Incorruption is life: is of heaven and eternal. A person who bears the image of Adam is corrupt and cannot ever escape death. Again, "like brings forth like;" no man can evolve into a god. Only the incorrupt can attain eternal life, and the only way to become incorrupt is to get rid of Adam's image and put on the image of Christ.

Romans
6:4 buried with Him by baptism into death. Old Adam must die. The baptism that Paul speaks of here is the death of our Adamic nature—the image of Adam dies when we are buried with Christ. **a new way of life.** Old Adam dies, and the Second Adam rises again. We put off the image of Adam in order to put on the image of Christ, rising again as He did to a new life that is free of corruption. Our flesh is still subject to death, because our flesh will always bear the image of Adam. We will still sin in the flesh and die in the flesh, since "flesh and blood cannot inherit the kingdom of God" (1 Cor. 15:50). But spiritually we have been made alive and will be resurrected with Christ.

8:1 no condemnation. This is the central point: we were condemned to die, condemned to be separated from God, because of Adam's sin. God's justice demanded this; it was Adam's decision to sin, so God was bound to let him die. Christ's death satisfied God's justice once and for all. He had not sinned and had no debt to pay, so He chose to pay our debt instead. **those in Christ Jesus.** The gift of eternal life only comes to those who have been born again, who have put to death the old Adam and put on the image of Christ. Until that decision is made, a person remains in the old Adam and under the condemnation of God's justice. It is as though as person were told that his debt had been paid in full, but he rejects the gift—such a person will still be in debt.

8:3 What the law could not do. The Old Testament law required that God's people sacrifice lambs to make atonement for their sins. This was only symbolic; an animal cannot pay for a man's sin. Nor can a man pay for his own sin; he is "limited by the flesh." So God Himself became the Lamb and shed His own blood to pay for our sins. "Without the shedding of blood there is no forgiveness" (Heb. 9:22). **in flesh like ours.** Jesus became a man so that He could pay for man's sin. He lived "under sin's domain," yet committed no sin. Therefore He was not subject to death, because He obeyed God rather than sin. The "law's requirement" was fulfilled by the shedding of blood that had no guilt or sin.

8:29 conformed to the image. When we are born again, we are born with the likeness of Christ. The likeness of Adam has died. **the firstborn among many brothers.** The first Adam had countless offspring, all bearing his image. So, too, will the Second Adam, and His image is eternal.

STUDY 06

What's with Different Religions?

SELECTIONS FROM OLD AND NEW TESTAMENTS

By this time the group has a good understanding of the basics of the gospel—that man has sinned and needs a savior. But sooner or later most young people will begin to ask why there are so many different religions in the world. Aren't they all more or less the same? Don't they all teach people how to be good and live good lives? Don't they mostly teach us how to find God?

Our modern culture has no shortage of false gospels. There are countless teachings available to our young people on what life is about and what comes next. In fact, these teachings are more than available; many are taught openly as truth in our schools and popular media.

It is helpful, therefore, to address the central question of how Christianity differs from other religions. We cannot provide an overview of the general teachings of all the world's religions in one study, nor would that be profitable. What is important is to grasp the central truths of Jesus' teachings, which we've been focusing on thus far, and to wrestle with His pronouncement that He is the only way to God.

This, of course, is the stumbling block for many. Our culture becomes outraged that anyone would dare suggest that there is only one way to get to heaven (if the concept of "heaven" is even permitted). Yet that is just what Christ claims: "No one comes to the Father except through Me"(John 14:6).

This is the short answer to the question about world religions. If you want to do business with Jesus, you must hear Him tell you that He is the one and only way to get to heaven. Other world religious systems might seem more tolerant of one another, allowing that they are just teaching one of many possible answers. But

Jesus will not sit passively when lies are being taught, and this truth is of vital importance to those who desire to find peace with God.

ACTIVITIES

Choose one of the activities below.

PARALLEL BLOCKS Using two identical sets of children's blocks, have two people sit back to back. Have one build a structure, while giving verbal instructions to the other. See how close the shapes are to one another.

GETTING TO KNOW YOU Pick 2 or 3 couples (guy and girl) who don't know one another well. Send them out to private areas for four minutes to get to know one another. Then bring them back into the room and separate the guys from the girls. Ask them a set of questions and see how well the couples got to know one another.

ICEBREAKERS

Choose one or two of these icebreakers.

>>> Who is your movie idol? Rock star idol? Sports hero?

>>> Have you ever had a near-death experience? What happened? What saved you?

>>> Tell us about when someone saved your life? Have you saved someone else's?

SCRIPTURE READING

Read the following passages from the Bible.

Exodus 20

READER ONE ² "I am the LORD your God, who brought you out of Egypt, out of the land of slavery.

³ "You shall have no other gods before me.

⁴ "You shall not make for yourself an idol in the form of anything in heaven above or on the earth beneath or in the waters below. ⁵ You shall not bow down to them or worship them; for I, the LORD your God, am a jealous God, punishing the children for the sin of the fathers to the third and fourth generation of those who hate me, ⁶ but showing love to a thousand generations of those who love me and keep my commandments.

Deuteronomy 6

READER TWO ⁴ Hear, O Israel: The LORD our God, the LORD is one. ⁵ Love the LORD your God with all your heart and with all your soul and with all your strength.

John 14; Acts 4

READER THREE ⁶ Jesus told him, "I am the way, the truth, and the life. No one comes to the Father except through Me.

¹² There is salvation in no one else, for there is no other name under heaven given to people by which we must be saved."

Acts 10; 1 Timothy 2

READER FOUR ⁴³ All the prophets testify about Him that through His name everyone who believes in Him will receive forgiveness of sins."

⁵ For there is one God and one mediator between God and man, a man, Christ Jesus,

⁶ who gave Himself—a ransom for all, a testimony at the proper time.

Galatians 1

`READER FIVE:` ⁶ I am amazed that you are so quickly turning away from Him who called you by the grace of Christ, and are turning to a different gospel— ⁷ not that there is another gospel, but there are some who are troubling you and want to change the gospel of Christ. ⁸ But even if we or an angel from heaven should preach to you a gospel other than what we have preached to you, a curse be on him! ⁹ As we have said before, I now say again: if anyone preaches to you a gospel contrary to what you received, a curse be on him!

Exodus 20:2–6 (NIV); Deuteronomy 6:4,5 (NIV); John 14:6;
Acts 4:12; 10:43; 1 Timothy 2:5–6; Galatians 1:6–9

DISCUSSION QUESTIONS

Select four or five questions from the head and heart sections, and/or make up your own.

>>> What does God mean when He says that He is "a jealous God" (Ex. 20:5)?

>>> What does it mean to love God "with all your heart and with all your soul and with all your might" (Deut. 6:5)?

>>> What does Jesus mean when He says that no one can get to God except through Him (John 14:6)? How does Jesus make that possible? Why is it that He alone can do this?

>>> What does Acts 4:12 mean, that there is "salvation in no one else"?

>>> According to Acts 10:43, who will receive forgiveness of sins? Who will not?

>>> What is a mediator (1 Tim. 2:5–6)? Why does man need a mediator with God? Why is Jesus the only one?

>>> Why do people seek religion in the first place? What do different religions promise?

>>> What does Jesus Christ promise?

>>> Are there other religions or philosophies that promise peace with God? Freedom from death? If so, how does a person attain those things?

>>> How is Jesus different from all world religions or "spiritual guides"?

>>> Does any other religious leader claim that he alone is the way to God? Does any claim that he is God? Has any ever risen again from the dead?

>>> Does it really matter if Jesus is the only way to God? If someone is sincere and kind, isn't that enough?

CARING TIME

Use all of these questions or make up your own.

Close with group prayer.

>>> How have you experienced the need for religion, a way to find guidance or help or forgiveness?

>>> How will you find true peace and life?

>>> Have you believed in Jesus? Or are you pursuing other ways of salvation? What are they?

>>> Would you like this group to pray for you today?

NEXT WEEK

This week Jesus confronted us with His challenge: "I alone can bring you peace with God." In the coming week, ask Jesus Himself to show you the way to peace with God. Next week, we will discuss what exactly it means to be "born again."

NOTES ON EXODUS 20.2-6 (NIV), DEUTERONOMY 6.4.5 (NIV), JOHN 14.6, ACTS 4.12; 10.43; 1 TIMOTHY 2.5-6, GALATIANS 1.6-9

Exodus
20:3 no other gods. A god is something or someone who is elevated to a level beyond our abilities that we turn to for guidance and protection and provision. This can take the form of an idol that one prays to, as with a statue of Buddha, or with a more subtle idol, such as the television.

20:5 a jealous God. God is very jealous of mankind's love. He created us in His own image so that we might love Him, but man's heart is perverse and we are constantly unfaithful. God's punishment of sin is always intended to regain man's love, not to inflict vengeance. He punishes sin "to the third and fourth generation" (v. 5) because children tend to carry on the sins of their parents. Yet He pours out His love to 1,000 generations—love is God's goal.

Deuteronomy
6:5 all your heart. This is the greatest commandment; it summarizes our whole duty toward God. Compare this with other world religions; many claim that our highest goal is to turn inward and find peace within ourselves, while others teach that we must obey some supreme being out of fear. The foundation of God's truth is that we must turn to God and be at peace with Him.

John
14:6 I am. There is only one way to God, says and that way is through Jesus. This is not a nice man teaching others to be kind and gentle; this is a very radical statement which still upsets people today. Jesus is telling us that only those who believe in Him will find peace with God; all others will die in their sins, no matter how they lived or what religion they followed. Our society today hates this message as much as the Pharisees did, preaching instead that each person must find his own way to God, if there is a God. In the name of tolerance all worldly religious

views are encouraged, yet the true hidden intolerance becomes clear when confronted with these words of Jesus. The world simply will not tolerate being told that Jesus is the only way.

Acts
10:43 everyone who believes. This gift of forgiveness is freely available—just believe the words of Jesus and be forgiven. The implication is that those who refuse to believe will never be forgiven.

1 Timothy
2:5–6 one God and one mediator. There is only one God. This defies most world religions of today. There is only one mediator—one Person who provides access. Many even deny that man needs a mediator, and they say since god is more or less a force and not a person that you only need to look inside to find your god.

Galatians
1:6 a different gospel. Paul was addressing a perverted version of the gospel which combined works with righteousness. Today's perversions are different, ranging from a mixture of new age philosophies and Christianity to completely different systems, yet the basic principle has not changed. Anyone who preaches a false gospel will be cursed.

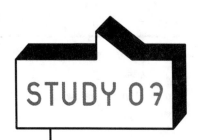

STUDY 07

So Now What?

We have come to our final study in this topic, and the pressing question must be asked: what will you do with Jesus? You can accept Him as Lord, receiving forgiveness of sins and eternal life, or you can reject Him and remain under the condemnation of God's righteous judgment. But you cannot simply ignore Him or dismiss Him as one of many religious teachers.

What comes now is a decision: will you be born again? This is the only way to see the kingdom of God, and it's a free gift of God's grace. All one needs to do is believe and confess.

In this study we will look at the Bible to find out just what it means to be "born again." We will see that it is simply a matter of faith, believing that Jesus was telling us the truth about who He is and who God is.

Do not hesitate to press the issue gently with your group. This is a very serious matter; it is literally a matter of eternal life or death. Each person is free to choose to receive Christ or to reject Him, but nobody should try to dodge the question by thinking that there are other options. There are no other options, and to pursue them is to reject Christ.

For those who do accept Jesus as their Savior, consider forming another Bible study group to continue on with other study guides in this series, such as Saltatiousness.

ACTIVITIES

Choose one of the activities below.

BALLOON RACE Divide into teams and give each person a balloon. The object is to cross the room first. As a relay, the first person on each team blows up a balloon and releases it. The next person starts where the first balloon lands and repeats until the team crosses the room and lands within a designated area.

SHEEP AND WOLVES Divide the room with a line of tape on the floor and have two wolves on one side and one shepherd and a bunch of sheep on the other side of the line. The sheep are blindfolded and the wolves each have a soft ball. The shepherd can block the ball or catch it. If the ball is caught the wolf is dead. If the ball hits a sheep, the sheep is dead. The shepherd can't die. No one can cross the line. After each throw the ball is returned to the wolf who threw it. The object is for as many of the sheep to survive as possible.

ICEBREAKERS

Choose one or two of these icebreakers.

››› Have you ever pretended to be excited about something in which you really weren't interested? What was it? Why did you fake it?

››› What was the greatest or most exciting piece of news you've ever gotten?

››› If you could be born all over again into a different family, what family would it be?

SCRIPTURE READING

Read the following passages from the
New Testament.

John 3

READER ONE ³ Jesus replied, " I assure you: Unless someone is born again, he cannot see the kingdom of God."
⁴ "But how can anyone be born when he is old?" Nicodemus asked Him. "Can he enter his mother's womb a second time and be born?"
⁵ Jesus answered, " I assure you: Unless someone is born of water and the Spirit, he cannot enter the kingdom of God. ⁶ Whatever is born of the flesh is flesh, and whatever is born of the Spirit is spirit."
¹⁶ "For God loved the world in this way: He gave His unique Son, so that everyone who believes in Him will not perish but have eternal life. ¹⁷ For God did not send His Son into the world that He might judge the world, but that the world might be saved through Him. ¹⁸ Anyone who believes in Him is not judged, but anyone who does not believe is already judged, because he has not believed in the name of the unique Son of God.

1 John 1

READER TWO ⁸ If we say, "We have no sin," we are deceiving ourselves, and the truth is not in us. ⁹ If we confess our sins, He is faithful and righteous to forgive us our sins and to cleanse us from all unrighteousness. ¹⁰ If we say, "We have not sinned," we make Him a liar, and His word is not in us.

2 My little children, I am writing you these things so that you may not sin. But if anyone does sin, we have an advocate with the Father—Jesus Christ the righteous One. ² He Himself is the propitiation for our sins, and not only for ours, but also for those of the whole world.

Roman 10

READER THREE ⁸ This is the message of faith that we proclaim: ⁹ if you confess with your mouth, "Jesus is Lord," and believe in your heart that God raised Him from the dead, you will be saved. ¹⁰ With the heart one believes, resulting in right-eousness, and with the mouth one confesses, resulting in salvation. ¹¹ Now the Scripture says, No one who believes on Him will be put to shame, ¹² for there is no distinction between Jew and Greek, since the same Lord of all is rich to all who call on Him. ¹³ For everyone who calls on the name of the Lord will be saved. ¹⁴ But how can they call on Him in whom they have not believed? And how can they believe without hearing about Him? And how can they hear without a preacher? ¹⁵ And how can they preach unless they are sent? As it is written: How welcome are the feet of those who announce the gospel of good things! ¹⁷ So faith comes from what is heard, and what is heard comes through the message about Christ.

John 3:3–6; 16–18; 1 John 1:8–2:2; Romans 10:8b–15, 17

DISCUSSION QUESTIONS

Select four or five questions from the head and heart sections, and/or make up your own.

>>> What does it mean to be "born again" (John 3:3)? What does it mean to be "born of water and the Spirit" (John 3:5)?

>>> What is Jesus referring to when He says, "Whatever is born of flesh is flesh" (John 3:6)?

>>> What does "propitiation" mean (1 John 2:2)? In what way has Jesus paid our debt?

>>> What does it mean to "confess with your mouth, 'Jesus is Lord'" (Rom 10:9)?

>>> What does it mean to "believe in your heart that God raised Him from the dead"? Why must a person do both (confess and believe) to be saved?

>>> How can a person gain eternal life?

>>> What does Jesus mean when He ways that anyone who does not believe is already judged (John. 3:18)?

>>> Has every person sinned? Why?

>>> What must a person do to become born again?

>>> How can Jesus change your life?

>>> What should a person do next after being born again?

CARING TIME

Use these questions or make up your own.

When you close in prayer be sensitive to the work of the Holy Spirit in your members. Be prepare to explain how to become a Christian.

>>> Would you like to be born again today?

>>> How can this group help you as you begin your new life?

>>> How can you tell others this week about the gospel of Jesus Christ?

NOTES ON JOHN 3:3-6, 16-18; 1 JOHN 1:8-2:2; ROMANS 10:8b-15, 17

John

3:3 born again. As we have seen, it is impossible for the flesh—the nature of Adam—to enter the spiritual kingdom of God. To do so, the old Adam must die and must be born again into the Second Adam's family.

3:5 water and the Spirit. Baptism symbolizes this death and resurrection. The old sin nature—the flesh—dies and is buried in the water; the new justified nature—the spirit—rises again to new life. In being reborn one receives the Holy Spirit, God's "down-payment" or "earnest" of His promise of eternal life in His kingdom.

3:6 flesh is flesh. Again, as we have seen before, Adam's descendants all bear his image, the sinful nature (or flesh) which is subject to death. One cannot serve two masters; you cannot be subject to (or serve) death and Christ at the same time. In order to be freed from bondage to death, one must die. This death, however, was accomplished for us on the cross.

3:17 judge. Jesus did not come to judge the world; God's judgment was already on the world. People were already subject to death—God's judgment—and Jesus came to set us free from that judgment. Those who reject Christ are already judged and are subject to death, but those who accept Christ will be set free from the judgment.

1 John
2:1 advocate with the Father. This is what we learned last week, that we have a mediator, a go-between, who stands between God and us. Jesus fills this position because He is both—God and man.

Romans
10:9 confess ... believe. Confession is a public declaration, an active choice. Adam declared that he would serve sin by eating the fruit. Belief is just that: believing God's Word. Eve believed the serpent rather than God, and her belief led to her action. If we believe that God raised Jesus from the dead, we acknowledge that He has defeated death and can therefore set us free.

NOTES

NOTES

NOTES

NOTES

NOTES

NOTES